GABRIEL FAURÉ

ÉLÉG

for Violoncello and Orchestra
Op. 24

Edited by/Herausgegeben von
Robert Orledge

Ernst Eulenburg Ltd
London · Mainz · Madrid · New York · Paris · Tokyo · Toronto · Zürich

GABRIEL FAURÉ

Élégie for cello and orchestra, Op. 24

Fauré composed his *Élégie* for cello and piano in 1880 for Jules Loëb, who first performed it at the Société Nationale in Paris on 15 December 1883, and this passionate and subsequently popular piece may have been conceived as the slow movement of a Cello Sonata that was never completed. In fact, Fauré often began sonatas thus, and the third period companion piece to the *Élégie*, the 1921 *Chant funéraire* for the centenary of the death of Napoleon I, provides a good example of this, as it became the slow movement of the Second Cello Sonata (Op. 117) later the same year.

Little is known about Fauré's orchestration of the *Élégie*, and the only surviving manuscript reveals that he needed help in its completion and originally had a more ethereal conception of the poignant, arabesque-like second theme (bars 24f and 45f) involving divisi and solo upper strings. The French Fauré scholar, Jean-Michel Nectoux, dates this orchestration at around 1895, though it could be slightly later as the *Élégie* was not performed with orchestra until 23 January 1902 in Monte Carlo, when the soloist was Carlo Sansoni and the conductor Léon Jéhin.

Editorial Notes

Sources

AUT   Autograph manuscript of the orchestral score, 22pp, Bibliothèque Nationale, Paris, MS 17751, *c.* 1895. Formerly in the collection of Mme Philippe Fauré-Fremiet.

SOLO   Hamelle first edition of the version for cello and piano (J. 2009 H), 7pp, Paris 1883.

HAM   Hamelle first edition of the orchestral score (J. 4718 H), 19pp, Paris 1901.

OP   Hamelle orchestral parts accompanying the first edition (J. 4719 H), Paris 1901.

AUT is an intermediate working manuscript which is unsigned, undated, untitled, and without a full prefatory stave or even a tempo marking. However, everything in black ink (the basis of the orchestration) is in Fauré's hand, and it is clear that he planned to use a larger orchestra than that found in HAM with two trumpets in F and 2 timpani at the climax (bars 35–8). The numerous pencil corrections and occasional comments in AUT show that Fauré asked for advice with his orchestration, possibly from more experienced friends like André

Messager or Camille Saint-Saëns, and this manuscript is thus of greater musicological than editorial value. It does, however, show that Fauré was most certain of himself with the climax of the *Élégie* (bars 32–44), and least sure in the final bars, which are extremely sketchy, even as regards the cello solo.

Neither the final manuscript used in the preparation of HAM nor Fauré's proof corrections for this have survived, but as HAM represents a considerable improvement on AUT, and as Fauré always checked his published editions thoroughly, HAM has been used as the basis of the present edition, with some help from SOLO and OP.

Editorial ties and slurs are in broken form and unnecessary precautionary accidentals have been removed, as have repeated accidentals or notes tied across barlines. Modern orchestral score layout has been restored and Fauré's woodwind phrase markings and orchestral string bowings have been retained throughout. Incorrect accidentals have been altered without comment.

Robert Orledge, 1981

GABRIEL FAURÉ

Élégie pour violoncelle et orchestre, Op. 24

Fauré composa son *Élégie pour violoncelle et orchestre* en 1880 pour Jules Loëb, qui en donna la première exécution le 15 décembre 1883 à la Société Nationale à Paris. Ce morceau passionné et par la suite très aimé du public peut avoir été conçu comme premier mouvement d'une sonate pour violoncelle inachevée. Fauré avait l'habitude de commencer ses sonates de cette façon: un bon exemple en est fourni par l'ultérieur morceau qui fait pendant à l'*Élégie*, le *Chant funéraire* (1921) à l'occasion du centenaire de la mort de Napoléon Ier, qui, plus tard dans la même année, devint le mouvement lent de la deuxième sonate pour violoncelle (Op. 117).

Fauré nous a laissé peu de renseignements sur son orchestration de l'*Élégie:* le seul manuscrit qui nous reste démontre qu'il ne parvenait pas à la compléter tout seul et qu'il avait eu une conception plus aérienne du poignant second thème en arabesque (mesures 24f et 45f) avec divisés et cordes supérieures en solo. Jean-Michel Nectoux propose une date vers 1895 pour cette orchestration: l'*Élégie* ne fut toutefois exécutée avec orchestre qu'en 1902 à Monte Carlo, avec Carlo Sansoni, soliste, sous la direction de Léon Jéhin.

Robert Orledge, 1981
Traduction de Genevieve Hawkins

GABRIEL FAURÉ

Élégie für Cello und Orchester, Op. 24

Fauré komponierte seine *Élégie* für Cello und Klavier im Jahre 1880. Sie war für Jules Loëb bestimmt, der diese Komposition erstmalig am 15. Dezember 1883 in einem Konzert der Société Nationale in Paris aufführte. Es könnte sein, daß dieses leidenschaftliche, später beliebte Stück ursprünglich als langsamer Satz einer unvollendet gebliebenen Cellosonate gedacht war. Tatsächlich entstanden Faurés Sonaten verschiedentlich auf diese Weise, und das Gegenstück zur *Élégie*, der *Chant funéraire* für die Hundertjahrfeier des Todes von Napoleon I aus Faurés dritter Schaffensperiode im Jahr 1921, ist dafür ein gutes Beispiel, denn dieses Stück wurde noch im selben Jahr als langsamer Satz in die zweite Cellosonate (Op. 117) übernommen.

Über Faurés Instrumentierung der *Élégie* ist wenig bekannt, und das einzige erhaltene Manuskript zeigt, daß ihm bei der Vollendung der Partitur geholfen wurde, weiterhin, daß das arabeskenhafte, lebhafte zweite Thema (Takt 24f. und 45f.) erst zarter gedacht war, und daß hier die Streicher ursprünglich geteilt waren mit solistischer Führung der höheren Streichinstrumente. Der französische Musikwissenschaftler und Fauré-Spezialist Jean-Michel Nectoux gibt dieser Instrumentation das geschätzte Datum 1895, jedoch könnte man es etwas später ansetzen, denn die *Élégie* mit Orchesterbegleitung wurde erst am 23. Januar 1902 in Monte Carlo aufgeführt. Carlo Sansoni war der Solist, Léon Jéhin der Dirigent.

Revisionsbericht: Allgemeines

Quellen

AUT   Autograph der Partitur, 22 S., Bibliothèque Nationale, Paris, MS 17751, *c.* 1895. Früher im Besitz von Mme. Philippe Fauré-Fremiet.

SOLO   Erstausgabe der Bearbeitung für Violoncello und Klavier bei Hamelle (J. 2009 H), 7 S., Paris 1883.

HAM   Erstausgabe der Partitur bei Hamelle (J. 4718 H), 19 S., Paris 1901.

OP   Orchesterstimmen zur Erstausgabe der Partitur bei Hamelle (J. 4719 H), Paris 1901.

AUT ist Arbeitsmanuskript in einem Übergangsstadium, unsigniert, undatiert und ohne Titel; es fehlen Instrumentenspiegel und sogar Tempovorschrift. Alle Eintragungen mit schwarzer Tinte, auf denen die endgültige Instrumentierung fußt, sind von Faurés Hand; es wird deutlich, daß Fauré ursprünglich ein größeres Orchester vorgesehen hatte, als es sich in HAM bei den Takten 35–38 des Höhepunkts mit zwei Trompeten in F und zwei Pauken findet. Die zahlreichen Bleistiftkorrekturen und gelegentlichen Anmerkungen in AUT belegen, daß Fauré beim Instrumentieren Rat einholte, möglicherweise von erfahreneren Freunden wie André Messager oder Camille Saint-Saëns. Auf diese Weise ist das Autograph für den Verleger von weitaus geringerem Interesse als vielmehr für den Musikwissenschaftler. Andererseits geht aus ihm hervor, daß Fauré sich beim Höhepunkt der *Élégie* (T. 32–44) seiner Sache völlig sicher war, weniger aber in den Schlußtakten, die nur skizzenhaft hingeworfen sind, als auch im Solopart.

Weder das endgültige Manuskript, das Stichvorlage für HAM war, noch Faurés Verbesserungen in den Korrekturabzügen waren endgültig. Weil HAM auf der Basis von AUT aber einen annehmbaren Kompromiß darstellt und Fauré seine Veröffentlichungen genau durchzusehen pflegte, wurde HAM der vorliegenden Ausgabe unter Hinzuziehung einiger Details aus SOLO und OP zugrunde gelegt.

Herausgeberzusätze erscheinen in eckigen Klammern; zugesetzte Bögen sind gestrichelt. Von Fauré eingefügte unnötige Vorsichts-Akzidentien sowie bei Überbindung über den Taktstrich wiederholte Akzidentien wurden ausgelassen. Die Anordnung der Partitur entspricht den heutigen Regeln; die Phrasierungszeichen Faurés in den Bläsern und seine Bogenstrich-Angaben in den Streicherstimmen wurden durchgehend beibehalten. Fälschlich gesetzte Akzidentien und offensichtliche geringfügige Abweichungen zwischen Analogiestellen wurden stillschweigend korrigiert.

Robert Orledge, 1981

Textual Notes/Einzelanmerkungen

1   HAM adds *Battez la croche* and has no dedication
15   Vc solo *molto cresc* AUT and SOLO. Accent on n2 in HAM only
18   Cl 2 *pp* from OP
30   Vc solo n1 down-bow mark and bowing slurs nn7–10 from AUT and SOLO, which
       have no slur joining nn1–3
33   Cor 1 & 2 dynamics from OP
34–44 String tremolandi in hemi-demi-semiquavers in HAM
37   Vc solo nn2–13 bowed as in AUT and SOLO. HAM has one continuous slur
38   Vc solo nn25–42, shorter bowing slurs restored as in AUT and SOLO
42   Vc solo nn1–2 bowed separately in HAM; slurred in AUT and SOLO
44   Vla I n8 a♭ in HAM; f in OP

À Monsieur Julës Loëb

ÉLÉGIE

Gabriel Fauré, Op.24
1845–1924

E E 6744   Edited by Robert Orledge
© 1981 Ernst Eulenburg Ltd, London

4

poco rit. | E | a tempo

12

14

E E 6744

15

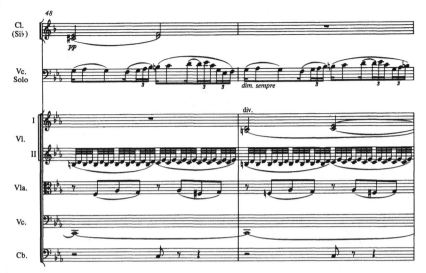

E E 6744